Talks That Sell

(Without Being Sales-zy or Weird)

by

Jan Saunders Maresh

DEDICATION

To my parents, Ray & Bernice Saunders who taught me how to work hard and with integrity. To my husband, Ted Maresh, and son, Todd Moser who support me unconditionally. Finally, to my clients who amaze me every day with their talent, brilliance, and desire to help make this a better world with what they do.

TABLE OF CONTENTS

INTRODUCTION

ACKNOWLEDGMENTS

I want to acknowledge Minesh Baxi and Eileen Gordon, business coaches who were all about getting me results and modeling what a good coach does for a client. You both showed me how to create a great business and one that makes a difference to me and each and every one of my clients.

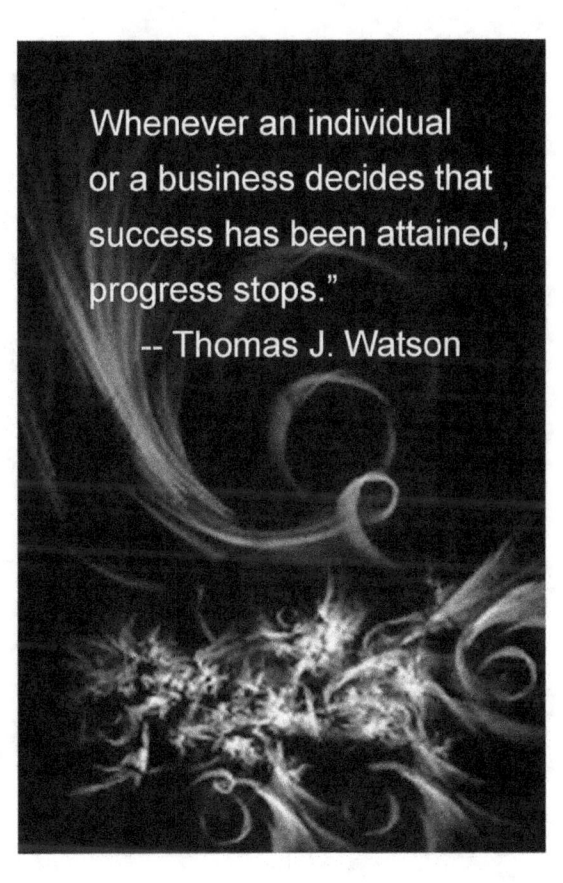

Whenever an individual
or a business decides that
success has been attained,
progress stops."
-- Thomas J. Watson

INTRODUCTION

Dear Creative Entrepreneur who's finally ready to earn what you're worth...

You may not know why you're reading this book right now, <u>but I do</u>. And I believe it's *no accident* that our paths are crossing at this moment.

Not only did you find this book for a reason, I'm absolutely certain that you found this **at a pivotal time in the life of your business**.

This sounds a bit out there, right? It's crazy to think that taking the few minutes to read this book could **dramatically shift the course of your business** for the better. But that's my bold promise to you.

If you have ever:

1) struggled to get **consistent clients and customers** flowing into your business (and who

hasn't?)

2) or struggled with your business & life balance –
specifically, leveraging the time you're having to
spend to generate enough revenue to survive – you
will be <u>extremely glad</u> you spent the next few
minutes reading this.

The most important thing I learned is as long as I
followed a **simple system**, I <u>never</u> had to worry
about where the business was going to come from
– ever again.

Over my 30+ year career I have adapted, refined
and applied this same system to other businesses
in multiple industries. I've sold books, physical
products and virtual products, all with similar
results because the system is proven.

It worked in a horrible economy, and **it works even
better now** regardless of the service or product
you're selling or your industry. Let me tell you
how.

1 CAN WE TALK?

If you had asked me a couple of years ago if I'd be writing this book, I would have said, "Why should I write something like that? Doesn't everyone just know this stuff?"

However, after watching so many business owners struggling to grow their businesses and working 60-80+ hours a week just to scrape by, I knew I needed to get this information out of my head and onto paper.

"Perpetual optimism is a force multiplier."
— Colin Powell

My goal here is simple. I want to show you how you can use <u>a proven, step-by-step method</u> to consistently get in front of your ideal clients *at will* so you finally achieve your greatest business goals -- all while **getting your life back**. Sound good?

My name is **Jan Saunders Maresh** and I'm the author of 17 books, including **<u>Home Staging for Dummies</u>** (1st, 2nd and 3rd Editions) as well as a Certified Trainer for the **CSP International Business Training Academy**. More importantly, I'm an award-winning sales and marketing expert who has been <u>exactly where you are right now</u>.

Wherever you are in your business, I've been there. From starting on a shoestring trying to get sales, to getting my business to crash through the glass ceiling; from hit-or-miss revenue to consistent cash flow, *I've seen it all*. In fact, I started my business at the worst possible time, and quite possibly under the worst possible circumstances.

> "Sometimes when you inno-
> vate, you make mistakes. It
> is best to admit them quickly,
> and get on with improving
> your other innovations."
> -- Steve Jobs

It Was The Early 80's

Several years out of college, I landed my second
corporate job. You know the regular paycheck,
expense account and paid vacations. But over the
next two years, it was apparent that the
department I started was costing the company
money, despite my Herculean efforts.

So I did the only thing that made sense to me at
the time and quit my job before being fired.

To make matters worse, unemployment was
around 8% and mortgage interest rates were a
whopping 14+% (you may even remember this). I
needed to do something **fast** or I was going to have

to move home with Mom and Dad and that just wasn't in my business plan.

No one was hiring. My savings account was running on empty, and, after three months, I didn't have a Plan B.

But ... I did have a friend whose company was hiring. She put in a good word, and, without previous experience, I got a straight commission sales job. Here was the kicker -- It wasn't until I got to training that I understood that I was also paying my own expenses and became a "reluctant entrepreneur."

And here was the kicker -- It wasn't until I got to training that I understood that I was also paying my own expenses and became a "Reluctant Entrepreneur."

What was I selling? School jackets to kindergarten though middle school kids (of all things). My first entrepreneurial endeavor – and unlike any job I had ever had, my income was now **100% my own responsibility**.   I know you understand what that's like.

Each day I traveled all over Central Ohio to different schools showing my school jackets at lunchtime to groups of kids who were far more interested in trading their bologna sandwich for peanut butter & jelly than they were in me.

I learned very quickly that if I wanted to pay my bills, I had to develop **a system** that would get their attention and peek their interest enough that they would order for a jacket.

So that's exactly what I did. Following a system, I perfected for giving a group talk that sells, over the course of the next 18 months I did just shy of...

$1,000,000.00 Dollars in Sales

Yes, you read that correctly: $1 Million Dollars in sales. (Actually it was $995,899.00 ... but you get the picture.)

Now let me be crystal clear. This book is <u>not</u> about me – **it's about you** and what's possible for your business by implementing the simple strategies that allowed me to make these sales happen.

You see, wherever you are in your business right now is a function is likely grounded in what you've been led to believe you "should" be doing to make your business successful. And it's entirely possible you've had a certain amount of success with whatever you're doing. Hey, it got you this far, right?

However, here's what you need to know. There's <u>a much easier way</u> to reliably get clients, customers and sales *without* working the 80-hour week and getting into the trap most business owners tend to fall into.

I'm here to tell you it's not only *possible* to achieve… but **probable** once you reframe how you approach what you're doing and follow some proven steps that I've honed over the past thirty plus years.

It actually begins with a foundation that may surprise you, but before I get into that, let's think about something for a minute.

2

Rush Of The Start-Up

Are you new to your business – or can remember back to when you were?

When I first started – reluctant entrepreneur that I was – I remember the energy and the excitement I felt every day. Everything was new, every answer was "yes" and it was exhilarating to be on such a huge learning curve.

I can remember moving on from school jackets to where I eventually found myself - working one-on-one with clients in the Home Staging industry. Every time a client would say, "I couldn't have done this without you," I wanted to hear it again. It sounds odd to say, but it was almost addictive to hear someone say that.

Sound familiar? Maybe at times (especially early on) you've felt a physical spike of energy or goose bumps which only affirmed that, "What I'm offering is really going to help this person."

This is the moment when you <u>knew</u> this is what you were put here to do. And the only thing that you cared about was how much **value** you were bringing to your clients.

Remember those days? As entrepreneurs that feeling is in every single one of us.

And then over time, **reality and survival hit.** Eventually you find that you're working so many hours that you've <u>lost yourself</u> inside your business.

Worse yet, you know you can help more people (and you <u>need</u> to do that to survive)... but **you <u>don't know</u> how to find them**.

Plus things start taking over. "Oh my gosh, I have to do the book keeping... I have to pay the taxes, I have to make enough to cover my rent or mortgage..." and it goes on and on.

And then, of course, there's this one: "You mean I need to *market myself* to actually get these clients so I can pay for all the other stuff?" At some point you throw up your hands and say, "I know exactly how to help these people, so why aren't they just *showing up*?"

You <u>know</u> what I mean – I know you do.

The result? Over time you start losing that spark you had in the beginning. You begin to lose your entrepreneurial juice – and you also start questioning your value. You wonder if being in your own business is everything it was cracked up (or you imagined it) to be.

"Comparanoia" creeps in.

- ✓ "Oh no, everyone else is more successful than me!"

- ✓ "What was I thinking by starting this in the first place?"

- ✓ "How can running this business be easier?"

The good news? There's a way out – and I'm going to show you how.

> ## "Good people go through the most bullshit."
> ### -- Tim Ferriss

By selling school jackets to kids I *accidentally* discovered a system that produces **a sustainable income** week in and week out, month in and month out. Without any previous selling or speaking experience in an industry I knew absolutely nothing about, I sold just under **$1,000,000.00** of a $20 product in 18 months.

So let's dig in. The next chapter is absolutely critical for you to **understand and embrace** if you want to make the system work for you.

Simply put, if you want a sustainable and thriving business...you can no longer rely on 1-to-1 Selling.

"The secret of business is to know something that nobody else knows."

-- Aristotle Onassis

3 Honeymoon's Over

It sounds dramatic to say, but in the current economy 1-to-1 selling is no longer reliable if you want your business to survive.

That's not to say that you'll never sell 1-to-1 again. In fact, you probably will. But, if you're selling a product, a service or you have a client-based business of any kind and you're relying on this as your main form of lead and revenue generation, you'll **never** climb out of the 1-to-1 rabbit hole. Why?

One-to-one selling is **too darn slow**.

Today's economy is all about *speed*, and most people just **are not ready to buy from you** the first time they meet you. It takes time for potential clients to get to know you well enough so they like you, and trust that what you offer is something that will actually help them.

But here's the other issue. In this marketplace you are competing with a lot of <u>distractions</u>.

If you currently rely heavily on 1-to-1 selling in your business, you've probably noticed it's become **a lot harder** to:

1) get the attention of your ideal customer type, and
2) to convert the folks from a lead to a paying client. (There's actually a specific reason for this that I will reveal to you later.)

At this point you're probably asking, "Alright Jan, if 1-to-1 selling is no longer the answer... then **what is**?"

Great question. The answer can be found in three simple strategies that form the exact foundation for how I was able to generate almost $1 Million in sales within 18 months... and how *you* are going to **completely transform your business** in the next 90 days.

It's All About the "Know, Like, Trust" Connection

Imagine this...

Next Monday you open your calendar and see that you have **six paying consultations** to do at $250 - $500 each.

Then, you open your email and see three **"thank you"** notes for the work you've done. And from those three emails you get another **nine qualified referrals** you believe will turn into business this month.

Sounds like a good week, doesn't it?

What if this happened every week – every month – and grew bigger **every year**?

How would it feel if you consistently got new clients, <u>bankable</u> consultations and you didn't have to market your business like you have been… PLUS you know you are **making a difference** in people's lives?

This is what happens when you decide to take action and do things differently – and implement a proven system that is based on your **"Know, Like and Trust Connection."**

A lot of business owners don't give much thought to the people they already know, who already like them and trust them – casually or not.

How about you?

Do you believe that the people you **already know** aren't in your target market?   Maybe you've tried asking for help from this group and come up empty-handed.

Or maybe (and this is a very common mistake) you just <u>assume</u> these folks know what your business is all about and **would naturally** call you when they needed your products and services.

Maybe you've been collecting contact information for a while now, don't really know what to do with it, and figure dealing with it will be *time-consuming*. Or maybe you're just procrastinating.

If so, that's okay – it's human nature! But remember this: Without a list of prospects, who are you going to **sell** to? Who are you going to *help*?

Without a continuous flow of qualified prospects, how is your **business going to stay afloat** and maintain sustainable growth? That's why you need a list. But that's only the start. So let's amp it up a bit.

A brand for a company is like a reputation for a person. You earn reputation by trying to do hard things well."

-- Jeff Bezos

4

Speak & They <u>Will</u> Come

Your list of contacts who already knows you, likes you and trusts you is what I call your **Power Circle**. Your Power Circle is a **living, breathing source of continuous business** (if nurtured and managed a specific way) that's filled with people who are making smart decisions about your products and services.

We'll get into the importance of **relationship building** with your list later, but for now, let's focus on building a quality list, okay?

The quickest way to put together Your Power Circle is to ask yourself a few questions.

Question 1: What is your Business Objective?

It's time for you to get clear on why **YOU want** a

working, breathing list. So ask yourself. <u>What are your business goals</u>? Here are a few to get you thinking:

- ✓ **BUILD my mailing list (database) for future marketing purposes**
- ✓ **TALK to my Power Circle**
- ✓ **FILL my revenue pipeline with paying clients**
- ✓ **START an online community centered on the services or products you offer**
- ✓ **GAIN VISIBILITY as an expert or resource in my field**
- ✓ **SELL more of what I offer to prospects, customers, and clients on a regular basis**

As you look this over you're probably thinking that you must do it all. But the key is that you **choose just one main** objective. Choose <u>one goal</u> that you can focus on. And then initially, **put all of your energy** and resources into that one goal.

Here's a suggestion. What is the <u>one thing</u> that will get **you in front of a targeted group of people**? When you know **that ONE thing** (which we'll get to

"If you work just for money, you'll never make it. But if you love what you are doing, and always put the customer first, success will be yours."

-Ray Kroc

shortly) everything else flows from there.

It will likely evolve as you and your business evolve, but your main objective will always be **the one goal** that keeps **you laser-focused** – and here it is.

Question 2: Who is your Target Audience?

So we're clear that you will use your list – your **Power Circle** – as a springboard to meet more people who want and need your services, but here's the thing…

You need to **know who they are**. The reason is because knowing who they are will **keep you focused** so you can connect better with your target audience that exists *within* your Power Circle.

Think of it this way. You've likely heard of "The Pareto Principle" – or as it's more commonly known, the 80/20 rule

The 80/20 rule states that approximately 80% of your business income will come from approximately 20% of your clients. The premise here is that 20% of your clients will always be your **best and highest-paying clients**.

That said, the power of this statistic actually has much larger implications for your success.

What if (and follow me here) there was a way to identify the 20% first, then gather them in **groups at a time** rather than just one at a time? And what if this target group ultimately becomes the core client of your business?

I call this *The 40/40 Rule*, which states this:

The 40/40 Rule

If you can <u>double</u> your Target Audience to 40%, then spend 40% attracting *just* those folks.

The other 20% of your time is now completely YOURS to use as you wish!

Isn't that why you started a business in the first place?

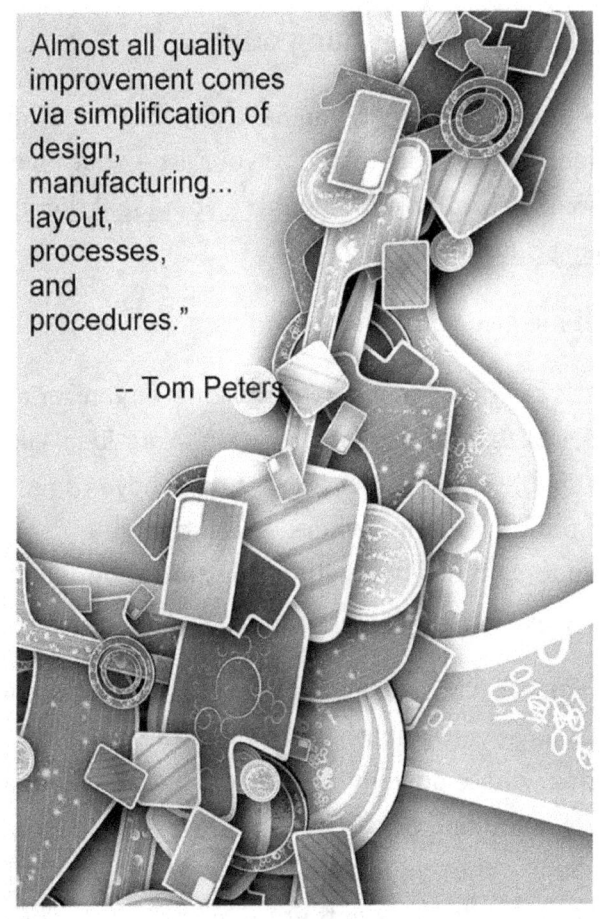

Almost all quality improvement comes via simplification of design, manufacturing... layout, processes, and procedures."

-- Tom Peters

Question 3: Where are they most likely to hang out?

As a business owner, you have a specialty. When identifying people to add to your list – Your Power Circle – also think about <u>where your ideal clients hang out</u>.

Let me give you some examples.

Let's say that you are a Professional Organizer and specialize in kitchen organization. Your ideal client probably likes kitchen gadgets, they have too many of them and **shop…where**? Besides online vendors, think about where **they are shopping locally**.

If you are a business coach, specializing in teaching clients how to publish and market their first E-Book, where do your ideal clients hang out online? When you find out, join their forums or Facebook groups. When you're part of that group, you make your presence known there.

And by watching what's going on. You also see what they want and can then tweak what you offer to fit what it is that will help them the most.

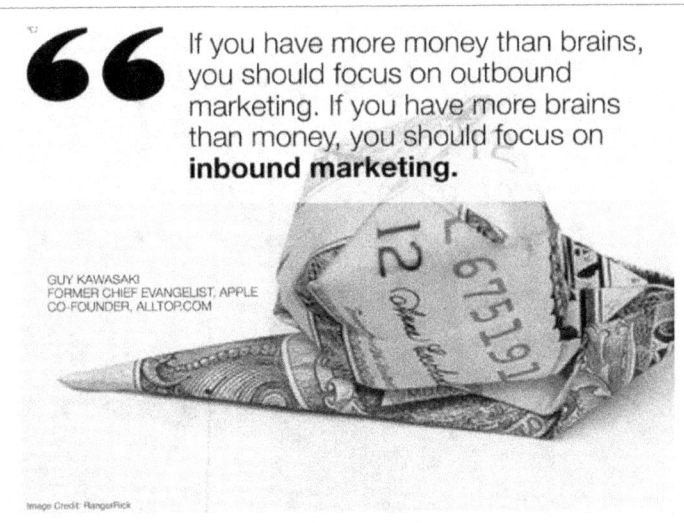

If you have more money than brains, you should focus on outbound marketing. If you have more brains than money, you should focus on **inbound marketing.**

GUY KAWASAKI
FORMER CHIEF EVANGELIST, APPLE
CO-FOUNDER, ALLTOP.COM

Image Credit: RangerRick

What if you specialize in creating online video content for other small businesses? Look at your Linked-In contacts. And for example, join some forums, read members' profiles and find where you might be able to plug some gaps in their marketing efforts with your video services.

Now that we've started to identify **who** you're going to talk to and where to find them, let's look at something you may have been avoiding – it's all about your numbers.

"The quality of a person's life is in direct proportion to their commitment to excellence, regardless of their chosen field of endeavor."

- Vince Lombardi

5 Own Your Numbers

As a business owner it's essential to look at your numbers. And before your eyes glaze over, I'm here to tell you that if you're serious about your business, if you're tempted to skip over this part... that line of thinking must **stop**. Today. Right now.

If you are an author, coach, Internet Marketer or Service Provider, <u>**your time has value**</u>. If you don't understand and honor that your time is valuable – and that you need to figure out your exact **Value Per Hour** (which I'll teach you how to do), then you are not a business owner... you are a *hobbyist*.

Granted, calculating your value per hour Is NOT the reason you got into the business in the first place, but **you need to know what it is**. If you don't, you won't know where you are at any given time and will end up spending your valuable time doing <u>non-income-generating activities</u> (and is the reason you've been struggling in the first place).

So how would you like it if you were able to look at your numbers, understand your actual **Value Per Hour**, and then bring this together in a way that will actually produce the results you want for your business?

When I was selling school jackets I had to manage my numbers every week – and I hated it. But when I took a closer look, **the numbers** told me where **I needed to focus my attention** and is where all the rest of the business flowed… all the way to $1 Million in sales.

There are two questions to examine for starting to uncover your Value Per Hour.

Question 1: What is your B.I.G.?

As business owners, we can over-complicate things, right? So ask yourself this.

What is the **one thing** you need to do **every day** to insure your **success**? The answer is your **Big Inspired Goal (B.I.G.).**

What's THE one thing can you do every day that

will both **inspire and lead** you to the results you want? **You need to** boil down this goal to its simplest form to give you the highest possible return.

When I was selling jackets, my B.I.G. was to give three **sales talks** a day. See? Simple! Just three sales talks a day was all I needed to do to start and keep the momentum going. Once I uncovered this goal using a simple formula and then simply <u>did</u> my three sales talks a day, I sold almost $1 Million of $20 jackets in 18 months.

"Too many people spend too much
time trying to perfect something
before they actually do it.
Instead of waiting for perfection,
run with what you got and fix it
along the way..."
— Paul Arden

Sounds easy right? So let me ask you another question...

Question 2: Are You Committed?

Before planning your next vacation with the money you're going to make, you need to make an **honest commitment** to **yourself**. You need to commit to **tracking your results** and taking a close look at those results **every week.**

As a business owner, you may find tracking your numbers every week tedious and may be tempted not to do it. So **find** an accountability partner – a friend, business owner with similar goals that you can **commit to**, or a business coach who will keep you on track.

It's kind of like having an exercising or dieting buddy. You'll be apt to take this seriously when **reporting** your results **to someone else**.

Don't want to share your financials? That's okay. Then track the **number of activities** you need to do to get you there. If your goal is to talk to three new prospects a day, track **how many phone calls or emails** you need to make a day to get there.

Whatever it is you need to do to reach your Big Impressive Goal – **that's what you track**. Then, once you commit to owning your numbers, there's one more strategy you must do.

Never sell to one when you can sell to a roomful of potential clients.

As business owners, we all have the same amount of time in a day to do our business. And we have to decide how to *leverage* that time.

So you're probably wondering, "What's the best way to leverage the time I have to devote to my business?"

The following strategy was what I learned selling my "silly school jackets" and that enabled me to sell just under $1,000,000.00 in 18 months. Are you ready for the next strategy? Here it is.

"Do more than is required.

What is the distance between someone who achieves their goals consistently and those who spend their lives and careers merely following? Go the extra mile."

-- Gary Ryan Blair

6

<u>STOP</u> Working So Hard ...

This is the secret right here. Bar none, the single most effective way to build and grow the business revenue you want in the current economy is to **gather and sell to a group of your target audience** versus selling to them 1-to-1. Why? Four reasons.

Reason 1: <u>Speaking To A Group</u> is THE FASTEST, CHEAPEST and EASIEST way to Connect and Build Relationships With Your Potential Clients

No one has really escaped the effects of The Great Recession. **And business owners like you have never been** in a better position to get your marketing traction back quickly and effectively.

How? By tapping into the connections you have in <u>Your Power Circle</u> – people who already know you, like you, and trust you.

First, you **don't** have to **invest in expensive** advertising campaigns to get business back on track. You **don't** have to **market one-to-one**. You don't even need to beef up your website or spend more time on Social Media.

"Perpetual optimism is a force multiplier."

-- Colin Powell

With everyone that's out there scrambling for **similar customers**, all you need is to be smart about it and have a well-crafted **Talk That Sells**. Period.

And before you freak out thinking that you can't do this, understand one thing.

Speaking is a skill that anyone **Can Learn Even If You Are Scared To Death To Get In Front Of A Group.** You just need to know how (more on that later).

Reason 2: <u>Speaking To A Group</u> Is The FASTEST, EASIEST and CHEAPEST Way to Fill your Revenue Pipeline

Think of this. When you set up opportunities to share your message with more people at once, you can **add those names** to your **database** and grow your list faster.

Here's exactly how this works:

- You tap into **Your Power Circle** to set up **group talks**.
- Your group talks get you **immediate business** with:
  - **paying** and free consultations, and
  - **referrals** to do more group talks.
- With each talk, you add more **qualified customers** to grow Your Power Circle.

- You use **social media** in a **targeted,** manageable way to keep in touch with Your Power Circle.
- Your Power Circle **thinks of you first** when they need your services.
- They **tell their friends** how great you are, growing your database even bigger.
- Your **revenue pipeline is filled**.
- You're **calendar** is filled with **moneymaking** activities.
- You can now <u>spend time on the activities that actually got you into the business</u> in the first place, just doing TWO well-crafted group talks a month.

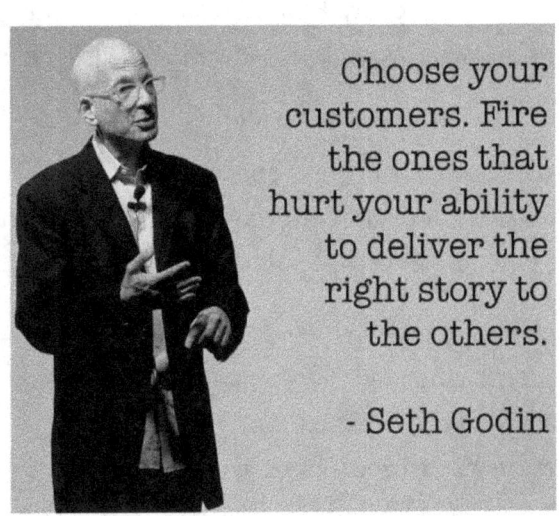

Choose your customers. Fire the ones that hurt your ability to deliver the right story to the others.

- Seth Godin

Reason 3: No One likes to Cold-Call!

As you know, most people **aren't ready to buy** from you the **first time** they meet you. It's **not personal ...** they **may not need** your service **right away** or realize that making an investment in your services will improve their life.

As a business owner, it's your job to keep your revenue pipeline filled, and it's so much easier when customers you're trying to reach are **referred to you by people they already know, like and**

trust. Finally, the <u>overall sales cycle takes less time</u> with a referral introduction. How might this look in your business?

Let's go back to our Professional Organizing example. In that example the **target customers** are people **who need storage solutions**.

You look over your current customer list and find **three clients** who want you to work your magic in other areas of their homes. You've **just added another service** to your menu and want to **get the word** out to as many people as you can. You also want to **find new customers**.

So you ask these **three clients** if they would host, for example, a **"Closets and Cocktails"** workshop in their homes for you.

In return, you **give them a discount** on your newest product or service and ask them if they would **share the experience** they've had working with you **with their friends**.

Each client invites their friends and family to a 1-hour workshop. Each workshop's average attendance is 15 (3 X 15 = 45). The results:

- You schedule **1 group talk a week** for **three consecutive weeks**.
- You talk to and **collect email addresses** from 45 people.
- 40 of the 45 are people **you have never met** and are potential clients.
- **10** people book a **paying consultation** at the workshops themselves (more on that later).
- Another **20 people** sign up for the **free 1-hour consultation**.
- You send out a personal **follow-up email** to the group inviting them to **visit your website** and sign up for your newsletter. This way you keep your name in front of the other **15 people** so when they need organization solutions, they **think of you first**.
- You book **three** more **Closets and Cocktails** workshops for next month.

Does this sound a heck of a lot better than cold-calling? **You bet it does.**

> "The majority of men meet with failure because of their lack of persistence in creating new plans to take the place of those which fail."
>
> -- Napoleon Hill

Reason 4: Speaking To A Group Positions You as <u>The Expert</u> in Your Field

There is a fundamental law of human existence about how we view what happens when somebody stands up in front of a room. Here it is.

We've been **conditioned since childhood** to respect the person who is standing up in front of the room and is addressing the group.

There is a unilateral shift that takes place when you stand up in front of a group because **your physical positioning** says, "I'm going to share some things with you and you're going to receive and listen."

When you're at the front of the room, you aren't better than anyone else, but <u>you automatically get authority, credibility, and establish yourself as THE Expert</u>.

And here's something else you need to know. Experts ALWAYS Earn More!

Why? The point of doing **Talks That Sell** is to close as **many qualified prospects** as possible **while you're standing right** in front of them.

Not only do you earn more immediately, **as you do your Talks That Sell – you become better known ... your Expert Status is elevated and people EXPECT to pay more for your services.**

7

If Not Now...When?

So let me ask you...

Are You Ready To Explode Your Business Results

... through a Powerful <u>Talks That Sell Process</u> – So You Can Leverage <u>Your Time and have the business</u> You Rightly Deserve and have always Wanted?

If the Answer is "Yes" I Have a *Valuable Invitation* to
Extend to You – But Only if You're Committed and <u>Ready</u>.

Over the course of many years I've worked to develop and systematize a duplicable way of not only creating <u>your</u> **results-based Talks That Sell**, but also getting it in front of **the exact people** who are waiting for it.

I've learned exactly what works when implementing this process – and more importantly, what *doesn't* work.

Based on incredible demand from readers just like you who have asked to learn more about exactly how this system works, I've put together a **online training** that you can attend <u>at absolutely no cost</u>.

The purpose of this training is to teach you how to begin **attracting groups of your Target Audience** using a proven <u>Talks That Sell Formula</u>, then show you what's possible for your business by sharing the talk consistently in a variety of venues.

> "Being good in business is the most fascinating kind of art. Making money is art and working is art and good business is the best art."
>
> -- Andy Warhol

<u>Important</u>: Only Results-Based Entrepreneurs Wanted

I'm choosing to share this method with a limited number of folks who are <u>totally committed</u> to adding **significantly more revenue to your business** with significantly *less time* invested.

That said, if you are someone who would prefer to keep doing what you're doing, I encourage you <u>not</u> to attend the training. And I do mean that.

However, if you're **100% dedicated** to exploding your business using the power of Group Talks **then you are someone I want to attend my online training.**

If you're finally ready to **join the TOP 1% of entrepreneurs** and spend more time actually doing your business than spinning your wheels <u>getting the business</u> – and if you're ready to create a **sustainable income** using a system I've spent 30+ years perfecting ... it's your time.

If you are <u>tired of sales rejection</u> and want **prospects** you meet to be **pre-sold** plus actually **want what you offer**, then follow this link and take the next step.

It's not only time...it's <u>your</u> time!

Go To

<u>www.TalksThatSell.com/</u>
<u>Talk-Training</u>

Your clients await!

"Content is KING but marketing is QUEEN and runs the house-hold."

— Gary Vaynerchuk

ABOUT THE AUTHOR

Jan Saunders Maresh, Author, Speaker and Group Talk expert teaches authors, speakers, service professionals and entrepreneurs to build sustainable businesses, by giving group talks where they actually sell something.

Early in her career, Jan became a Reluctant Entrepreneur and discovered a "Talks That Sell" sales Formula she used to generate $1 Million Dollars in personal sales within just 18 months – starting from scratch.

Over her career, she perfected this system and sold everything from books, decorating products, design services – even virtual products – all using the same simple sales process.

As a Home Shopping Network pitchman and best-selling "For Dummies" author, Jan now combines her sense of humor with her award-winning marketing savvy to train passion-driven business owners how to give Talks That Sell -- even if they're scared to death to speak to a group.

She says her most impressive career achievement has been, mastering the challenge of creating and running a sustainable one-person service business.

"When I figured out how to get off that "Revenue Roller Coaster" by giving a strategically designed Group Talk and then generated a sustainable income doing what I love, that's when I knew I needed to share this system with other like-minded professionals. I've made all the mistakes…so they don't have to."

In late 2014, Saunders-Maresh launched Talks That Sell. To market her company and expertise she teaches several online classes and speaks at national and local industry events.

Jan is the proud mom of their rocket-scientist son (yes…he's actually a rocket scientist). She's also madly in love with her husband of 24 years and they live in Longmeadow, MA with their adorable rescue, Polly. Her favorite things are her sewing machine, almost anything mid-century modern, dark chocolate, and everything her husband cooks. For more on Jan visit www.TalksThatSell.com.

Book Jan Saunders Maresh to Speak at your next meeting or event

... and Grow Your Business

Jan conducts her compelling presentation for groups of small business owners who want to grow their businesses by getting more clients and who want to sell more of their products and services.

Depending on your format, the time available, and your meeting objectives her presentation can be run from 30 minutes to three days. It zeros in on the core issues that business owners face on a daily basis ... and so the focus is on how to get more prospects, more referrals and ultimately more sustainable business!

For availability and booking information you can reach Jan at jan@TalksThatSell.com or call her direct at 360-903-8976.

This is NOT Good Bye ...

Share *Talks That Sell (Without Being Sales-zy or Weird)!* with your friends, family members and colleagues. Buy 25 copies and get a 25% discount. Email me at jan@TalksThatSell.com for special pricing on larger qualities.

Send me your comments. I would like to hear your success stories, insights, and any ideas for future reference and additional books. So again, send an email to me at jan@TalksThatSell.com.

Then, please go to www.TalksThatSell.com. It's a great place to find tools for authors, speakers, business owners, entrepreneurs, and service providers who want to grow their businesses and perform at their best.

It takes a team. A big Thank You goes out to my family, friends, and clients that have helped me get this book done and offer unwavering encouragement to my mission. Your faith in me and support of my work has surpassed my wildest dreams.

Your clients await,
Jan Saunders Maresh